OUT OF THE QUIET DARK

OUT OF THE QUIET DARK

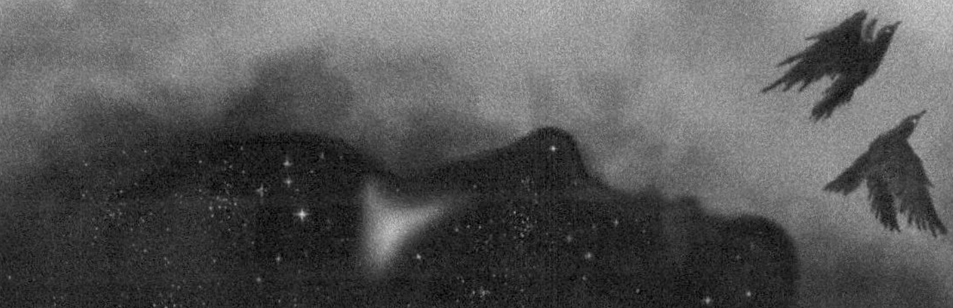

KAYLA S. COOK

Out of the Quiet Dark

For information about this title, contact the publisher:

CROW MOON FIELDS

Crowmoonfields.com

ISBN: 979-8-9950312-0-8 (softcover)

Printed in the United States of America

Cover and Interior Illustrations: Kayla S. Cook

DISCLAIMER

The poems within this collection relate to themes many may find uncomfortable, including trauma, PTSD, depression, suicide, domestic violence, and abuse. While some poems may be comforting, many may be triggering.

This collection is composed of rhyming and non-rhyming poetry, which may be off-putting for some people. Those who tend to like rhyming poetry often dislike non-rhyming poetry, and vice versa. This won't be everyone's cup of tea, and it isn't meant to be.

I deliberately mixed the poetry to be unsettling. Trauma can change us in ways we can't anticipate. It can disrupt our natural flow, lead to inconsistencies in behavior and thought, and cause us to spiral into madness. Even when we begin to overcome our trauma, it can sneak up on us and drag us back down when we least expect it. That doesn't mean we can't get back up again.

Similarly, these poems can be unpredictable. They jump around a bit in execution, topic, and tone. To me, the setup of this collection mirrors the disruption and inconsistencies that trauma has introduced into my life and the lives of others I have interacted with. This collection is meant to be disturbing, raw, and unfettered—even jarring. Please keep that in mind as you proceed.

TABLE OF CONTENTS

DUSK

Blood red sunlight spills
through the crisp, darkening leaves—
light birthing darkness.

Now day turns to night,
stirring shadow-steeped nightmares
amidst autumn dreams.

NESTING DOLLS

Doorways yawn wide
like open wounds in plaster skin.
Little deaths are scattered
about the house:
Shattered glass on cracked
tile and smashed TVs.
Holes in walls, locks dangling
like snapped arms on doors.
Horrors in the shadows, unsafe,
nowhere to run, trapped—
in all the broken homes.
Screams reverberating within
differently gilded cages.
Ghosts in the shell, nesting dolls
wrapped in layers of despair.
Flesh cracked like porcelain,
crazed with pain,
shades drawn over wet eyes.
Only to be assaulted by the damage
within, screaming on the inside.
Words replayed over again, twisting
blades, solidifying insecurities.
Houses, families, loves, bodies, minds—
one broken home after another,
nesting dolls whose blood
chokes one another.
We all have darkness in our past.

Some of us still live it.

SHADES AND NIGHTMARES

There was soul-crushing terror,
screams from below,
blood on the floor,
dying hope.

Years of betrayal, over and over again,
wondering who would kill whom.
Broken promises and tearful
goodbyes.

Hands doing things hands shouldn't,
threats whispered like
honeyed promises.
Pain.

Memories return in nightmares,
sleep paralysis, cries in the night;
some nightmares are broken dreams
that just didn't heal right.

Other nightmares are flesh, bone, and blood,
human in the loosest sense of the word.
Male, female, makes no difference;
the pain inflicted is the same.

PTSD

Pay attention to the signs.
Take a close look into the beyond.
Shattered glass, seething torment inside.
Darkness, deep beneath the apathetic mask.

THE BATTLE

There is a monster under my bed
in the darkness, in my head.
I created it from rage and fear,
to protect me through each helpless year.
But now it's going too far and I wonder,
which of us is real, which is stronger?

DEAD OF WINTER

Winter falls over the land,
allowing none to take a stand
against its cold and icy breath
that promises only fear and death.
Watch how it freezes the lakes and streams.
Watch how it stifles the sun's golden beams,
brings its darkness down on all living things,
and halts the beating of the angels' wings.
Winter can be a monster in itself.
Worse still is when it's taken into oneself.

MONSTER'S LULLABY

I'm the monster, but not the cause of your woe:
I am YOUR monster, and yours alone!
I'll be the one to make your enemies atone.

I am the devil in the darkest night,
I am the cold, cold wind on your enemies' faces.
I am the freezing thrill, why your heart races.

But I can be the angel in disguise,
I can be warm, I can be sweet,
the moon's soft glow, the sun's burning heat.

My sad, lonely host, don't be scared—
talk to me, leave others as they are.
I'll heed all you say and accept every bar!

And from my cage I'll serve you forever.
I'll be here for you, here to stay,
here to chase all other demons away.

While I devour your heart and mind,
while I worm my way into your soul,
while you think you're in control.

WHAT DARKNESS IS THIS?

What darkness is this,
that creeps into our rooms at night,
sneaking and slithering
around each shred of light?

What darkness is this,
this silent, unnerving force,
that grabs us in waking nightmares
and drags us somewhere worse?

What darkness is this,
and will it go away?
Will it let us live in peace?
Why can't our light keep it at bay?

Oh, God help us.
What darkness is this?

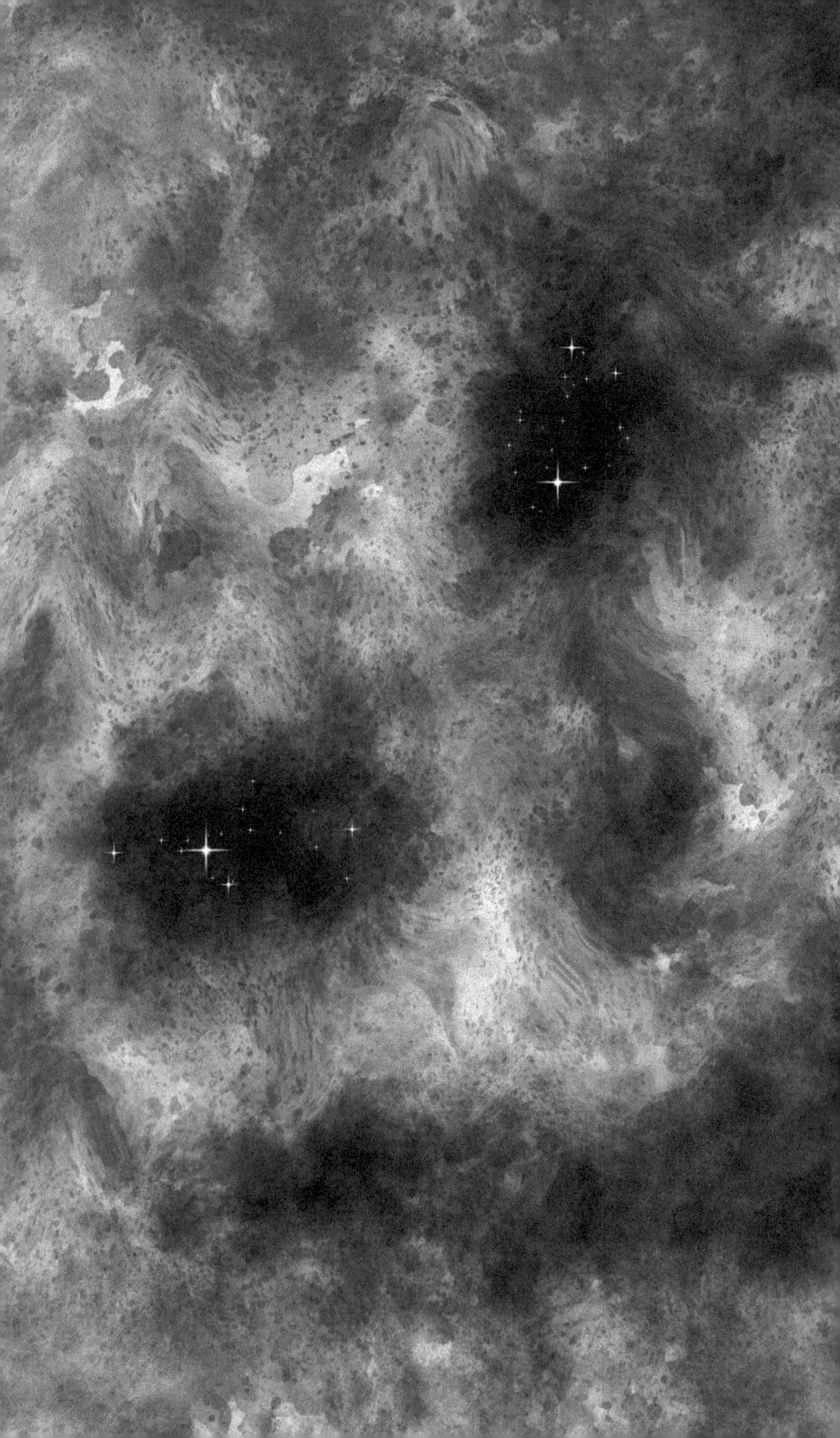

THE AMORPHOUS DARK

Come lie down upon your bed.
Come rest your battered, weary head.
Close your eyes, open your soul
to the darkest dreams, the waiting ghoul.
Slip away unseen, unfelt
through that thin veneer, that fleshy pelt.
Slide on down to our dark palace;
you've drunk the wine, now refill your chalice.
We've been waiting so long right here,
beneath lucidity and all its sorrow and fear.
Don't fear our dark, don't fear our cold.
Don't remember what you were told.
We are the amorphous dark, the shifting light,
not bound by shape, not held by your sight.
What are we, but reflections of what is?
What are we to you, yours or His?

COME AND SEE

Come, my dear, come and see
the darkness deep inside of me.
Come on down where no one goes,
see if you can heal my woes.
Take my black heart in your hands,
turn it white as moonlit sands.
Mend my soul, steal my pain
hear my cries, make me sane.
Lead me from this darkened field.
Hide me behind a heavenly shield.
Remember how I used to be,
long before I drowned at sea—
that dark, dark sea of fear and death
that swallowed me whole and stole my breath,
that filled my heart, my lungs, my soul
with misery, pain, war, and gall.
Be my angel, savior, light my way
and I'll keep you safe throughout each day.
Be my balm, my guide, my friend,
but turn on me once and you'll meet your end.

MY DEEP, DARK SEA

If I let you pick through my soul
how far down would you dare to go?
Would you dive deep into the ocean of my heart,
hoping to find some treasure with which to depart?

I assure you there is much I buried there
in the nooks and crannies of my hidden lair.
Oh, there're jewels and pearls and gold aplenty!
Help yourself, leave my heart dark and empty.

But beware: Where darkness is, so, too, are monsters,
and there are many in my stormy waters.
They'll let you down to that dark lair,
but they'll never let you escape—not one hair.

WHERE THE MONSTERS GO

This is where the monsters go
when the sun rises from an all new low.
They slither deep down into the heart
and burrow into its darkest part.
The monsters cry and scream and shake
until day falls under night, and will and resolve break.
When dark deeds are done and battered conscience returns,
the mind clutches to what each monster spurns,
and order returns until next nightfall,
when the monsters escape again and overcome all.
And with each outbreak, the conscience dies more and more,
until the owner feels no more, no more.
But we can fight them if we try.
We don't have to be what we despise.

LATE WINTER TEARS

Sorrow has a savage beauty in its honesty.
Unmasked, raw, relentless, raging—
a river bursting from the frozen confines
of wintry perfection and numb indifference.
The snow melts, the clouds part,
and the ruthless sun reveals the remains
of past kills, decaying flesh, shattered dreams.
Acknowledging the pain and wrongness
starts the path to clearing the corpses,
and letting go of the torment screaming inside.

THERE MAY BE A LIGHT

There may be a light up ahead,
something to guide the living more than the dead.
There may be a light around that bend,
some kind of blessing or Godsend.
There may be a light on down this road,
some shred of peace or stable abode.
There may be a light up ahead…
or just a fool's hope for a sun long since fled.

THE DARK FOREST

At midnight many years ago
when I was still a child
I walked along a trail at night
through old woods dark and wild.

That trail I walked, I walked alone
and I never once complained,
for the loneliness, it suited me
and within me that solitude reigned.

I liked the woods at that late hour
because I saw myself in their dark depths.
Those woods were me, and I was them;
we shared a darkness still no one accepts.

We liked it quiet as the grave,
we liked it dark as blackest night.
We liked it when there were none around,
when we were hidden in the shadows, out of sight.

Those trees and I, we preferred it that way,
in that stark gloom where shadows roam,
because no one else would come out at night,
and the trees shared secrets unrecorded in any tome.

(continued on next page)

(continued from previous page)

They spoke of things unspeakable.
They whispered of dark deeds past.
They sang of torture, murder, and betrayal,
and showed me how love is rarely allowed to last.

They bent their boughs and showed me where
ropes and wire had left their scars.
They unearthed their roots and let me see
the bones that lay beneath those wooden bars.

That walk through night taught me much
about life and death and what happens when
one speaks her mind or raises his fist
to those unfair, cruel, and steeped in sin.

Knowledge is both a blessing and a curse,
and though those without it can fly so very high,
so many find themselves shot down one day—
I never flew as high as they, but all the same, fallen am I.

YOU

When I needed help, you
shunned me and
called me a liar and
threatened me and
tried to silence me.
You pretended everything was
all right and normal and that
I was the one with the problem.
I've been told how lucky I am,
and maybe I am lucky—
certainly luckier than most.
But don't try to invalidate and
belittle my pain because of your
own laziness, fear, or guilt.

GOD, I'M ANGRY

Forgive me, Lord, but I am angry.
I hate the way the world is,
what we do to each other.
I know we have free will.
We're either the victims of our
own choices or the choices of others.
But free will is overrated.
It allows us to stray and stumble.
If only we were your puppets,
this world would be a better place.
Instead we have autonomy,
and that's a greater responsibility
than most of us can handle.
I know we have a conscience.
I know you try to guide us through it.
I wish more of us listened to that

quiet, soft voice in our heads—
the voice that warns us away from
danger, from temptation, from evil.
More of a feeling than a straight message.
We don't need to go to church to find you.
You're always there. You live in us.
Yet most ignore you to the point
that it's as if you aren't in them at all.
Some people seem to have no conscience.
So, I'm angry.
Not at you, but at the world.
And at myself.
Because if WE all put in the effort,
we could turn this world around,
make it a better place for everyone.
But too many of us don't.

GRAVITY

How far to fall through winter's squall. . .
How long to wade through misery's glade. . .
The pain of the world, now unfurled,
descends upon us and crushes the just.

THE NIGHT QUEEN

There was a feral cat on my porch the other night,
her sleek body stretched out along the step.
Such was not the place for so fine a creature,
yet there she was all the same.
She held herself as if she had no care at all,
and yet it seemed
a great weight was nestled in the hollow
between her hackles.
I wondered if other cats noticed it, too,
or if they just passed by,
oblivious, envious shades in the night.
She stepped off the porch with a royal grace,
blue-gray head held high,
furry tail carelessly erect.
Her poise was so flawless that
I almost didn't notice the ribs poking
through her loose hide or
the matted fur of her belly.
This Night Queen sauntered off,
doing her utmost best to hide
her pain from the world.
I bid her a silent farewell,
understanding well her struggle.
Appearances must be kept up lest
our weakness be used against us.

(continued on next page)

(continued from previous page)

A few days later, I saw her
lying on my porch again,
and I was happy I had put milk out that morning.
But she didn't touch the milk,
didn't move for a whole day.
She hadn't lost her grace.
Though stiff, she looked no less formidable.
So complete was her power
and mastery over appearances
that not even the vultures bothered her.
But I knew better. We recognize our own.
As I reverently pick up her body to bury it,
I imagine the other cats picturing her
ruling over finer courts than this neighborhood.
Would they ever guess,
in their jealousy and awe,
that in the new lands she'd left them for,
only the worms marvel at her decaying splendor—
that the Night Queen is no more?

ONE-SIDED

"Hello again!"
…
"Oh, nothing much. I just wanted
to see how you were. Last time we
talked, you weren't doing so great,
so I just wanted to check in again."
…
"That's great to hear."
…
"Oh, you're welcome. You know
I'm here for you, like I've always been.
Since all is well, I guess I'll let you go—"
…
"Oh, me? I'm…fine."
…
"Yes, really."
…
"Of course, I know you're here for me."
…

(continued on next page)

(continued from previous page)

"Well, I guess there is something bothering me. It would help to talk to you about—"

Line disconnects.

"Hello?"

Silence.

"Are you still there?"

Silence.

THE WORLD WEEPS WITH ME

The sky weeps upon the shattered walkway,
soaking the cracked pavement with its tears,
churning the lake water into a murky mess.
Puddles form here and there, reflecting the
sky's pain back up to its azure countenance.
In my room, alone and small, I shed my own.
They spill from my eyes and slide down my face,
the trails they leave as invisible as my worst scars.
They collect at the razor edge of my chin before
falling to meet the faded pages of my story.
Splat,
Splat,
Splat—
Fall the tears on both sides of the foggy window
that faintly reflects my frail features back to me.
As I sit in my room, the world weeps with me.
Together we let our pain water the seeds of our future,
hoping for something better but knowing the soil is sour.

REMEMBER ME WHOLE

Remember me as I was,
when I was younger in soul
and clearer in mind.
I was not happy then, either,
but I was whole.
If I could scrape up the pieces,
fit them all back together,
I would,
but many are lost and
it's too easy to cut myself
on the edges of those that remain.
So instead, I ask of you a simple favor:
Remember me—the real me,
the me of flesh and bone,
the me of light and love.
Remember me whole
and, at least in your memory,
I will be again.

LIFE OR DEATH

I've had more than one person
ask me why I don't just up and die.
At my lowest moments, I sometimes
ask myself that same question.
Life is hard, and it's natural to
reach a point where you just want
to lie down and slip away from
all the worries and concerns.
Death doesn't seem so bad sometimes.
But the more I think about it—
about slipping away—
the more I realize I'm just not ready.
I'm tired of the way my life has been,
but I don't actually want to die.
I just want to finally, truly, wholly live.
And it's about time I do something about that.

REACHING OUT

I reach out with my words—
simple lines scribbled on stark white sheets,
whispered on soft, time-silvered breaths,
shrieked from soul-deep shadows and light—
severed from my heart of hearts
to sail, skip, seep, slip into yours—
or try.
Whether scribed, sighed, or screamed,
my words seem to strike the same walls
again and again, never allowed entry.
Or maybe they speed into the void of space,
lost amidst all the other signals.
Still I reach out, spanning the space between,
seeking you out with speech and those
scrawled stains on slippery pages.
One of these days, I'm sure my words
will get through to you, kindred spirits,
dearest friends, those who I have yet to meet
and those who have slipped out of reach.

WILL YOU BE THERE?

Will you be there when I die,
take my hand and fly me high?
Pull me from a sleep so dark,
guide me along the tune of the lark?
Lift me from my sea of pain,
catch me if I fall again?

Will you be there when I pass,
when my soul is free at last?
Toss me a lure, throw me a rope,
so I have something on which to base my hope?
Sing me a song, return my heart,
save me from myself, never again depart?

Will you be there when my life fades,
when I reach my end of days?
Grab my soul or give me wings,
help me find where that lark sings?
Teach me to fly, help me to soar
until my wounds don't hurt me anymore?

If I die tonight will you take me
to where you've been these past few years?
If I sleep and decide not to wake
will you pull me from my fears?
Or will you meet me in a dream and ask me to stay
here in this world of pain and this body of clay?
Can I visit you again
in dream or death or thought or glen?
Can I feel you in my arms again,
my dearest, sweetest, long gone friend?
Or will my nights be dreamless, my life too long,
my memories lost, or my world too wrong?

Say I can look forward to seeing you once more,
and I'll wait to pass through Heaven's door.
You give me the time, promise to be fair,
and I'll be sure to meet you there.
Anything less would be too much to bear.
Will you be there?

ASCENSION

Let's run away together, run back in time,
ride the light to someplace warm and bright
where there's no more fear or pain.
Create a new world; forget this half-life, living-death.
We'll exsanguinate Time, take back what's ours,
make us younger—me, a child in your arms again.

Yet will we find new life nearly as precious without the pain?
Did we know then what we know now,
or was it all taken for granted until the end?
Perhaps it would be better to build up from where we stand,
grow from our pain, burn our enemies in our phoenix-flames,
scatter their ashes with each beat of our wings.

Let's finally live, something we haven't done since birth;
kill Death and deal Pain a wound of its own.
Let go of these monsters, rattle these living corpses,
climb out of our graves before any more dirt is thrown on us.
Let our rage shake the death-shroud from us, our love lift us up—
let's rise from our prison cell and fly away.

DIRGE OF THE FOUND

An early morning prayer,
a nightly flood of tears,
a growing sense of fear that makes
all my thoughts unclear.

Fear that I'll never
be free of this pain
that rips right through my body,
my heart, my soul, my brain.

Watch without seeing this pain that's never leaving.
Hear without heeding the war drums in me beating.
See the rays fall under the darkening of the sky.
See the sky within my being darken as they die.

Is there a way to finally
fly back up into the light,
out of the pain
that never seems to want to go away?

The early morning prayer,
the nightly flood of tears,
the growing sense of fear
that makes all my thoughts unclear.

All of these combine
to keep me tied up, in a bind
that I won't be able to break
without crossing over the line.

Watch without seeing the soul within me grieving.
Hear without heeding the darkness in me seething.
See the darkness spreading; see the light retreat.
See the ground get stolen out from underneath my feet.

There is a way to finally
fly back up into the light,
out of the pain
that never seems to want to go away.

The early morning prayer,
the nightly flood of tears,
one has ceased to flow, the other
has finally drowned out my fears.

Fears that won't ever
tear at me again;
fears that won't ever
creep along beneath my skin.

Watch now and see the darkness in me leave.
Hear now and heed the bugle cry—take the lead.
See the demons flee; see the light break free.
See the darkness fall down far beneath the sea.

I found the way to finally
fly back up into the light,
out of the pain
that never seemed to want to go away.

TOMORROW

When I wake up tomorrow, I
am going to get out of bed.
I will rise to face the day.
Even if that's my only
accomplishment,
I think that's a good start.

BABY STEPS

I stumbled, trying to fly before I learned
to walk again. I was so impatient
to build a better life,
I forgot to take baby steps.
I forgot to set smaller,
obtainable goals to build
myself up, strengthen myself.
And I stumbled. Bit off
more than I could chew.
I felt that old familiar darkness
creeping back in, threatening
to pull me back under,
and then, that small,
quiet voice inside me
told me it would be okay.
Because tomorrow is another day
and I am no longer afraid to try
again. Believing is part of
the battle, and I believe
anything is possible.
As long as I keep trying.
As long as I keep praying.
As long as I keep planning.
And once I've tried and prayed
and planned enough, I'll take
action, and then I'll fly and
nothing will be able to
hold me back anymore.
One day.

OCEAN SONG

I've only seen the ocean once,
and while my memory has faded,
I can still hear the crashing waves,
the roar of power unevaded.

There's beauty in the wild tide,
hope in that expanse of mirrored sky.
Everything has a song of its own,
and I still recall the ocean's lullaby.

One day, I may return to see if I
can find where sky and ocean meet.
Then I'll claim my place along the shore,
where wind, water, and my heart shall beat.

DAWN: A NEW DOOR OPENS

Softly I feel it stirring
deep beneath my skin,
under frost and darkness,
beyond their remembered sin.

Out of pain and fear it seeps,
unfurling rays of light.
Through icy blood it creeps,
shattering my eternal night.

Numbness fades and life returns,
silent eventide recedes.
Dawn breaks anew and brightens all,
sorrow slowly leaves.

Compassion thawed my heart,
awakened me once more.
A little kindness and hope go far.
There is love above, and an open door.

AUTHOR'S NOTE

This poetry collection was at once a labor of love and hate. I wrote these poems over the course of several years, starting in 2012. They've gone through many revisions, and most of them have grown with me, changing with my shifting emotions and attitudes. I love writing poetry. I don't love all the emotions that fuel it.

My mother helped inspire and cultivate my love of writing and art. These quickly transformed from hobbies into lifelines. Art (of all kinds) has long been a means of therapy for me. It allows me to express my emotions in an artistic, creative way. As such, many of the poems found within this book are raw with emotion.

All art is subjective. While each poem in this collection has a specific meaning to me, they may have different meanings for others, and that's all right. For me, these poems tell a story of dealing with trauma and attempting to overcome it. They may or may not resonate with others. Everyone responds to trauma in their own way.

I've read many poems over the years, and it's always the darker poems that resonate with me most because they help me feel like someone understands where I'm coming from. Along that line, my hope is that others who've experienced various forms of trauma (let's face it—most people have) will be able to connect with at least a few of these poems and feel a little less alone.

Throughout the years, I've learned that I can't control everything that happens, but I can (with practice, patience, prayer, and help) control my thoughts, attitude, and actions. I can choose to dwell on the pain or to dwell on my future. I didn't always see it that way. I'm still a work-in-progress, but I've come a long way. Writing and reading poetry helps.

There are also quite a few people who reached out a helping hand in one form or another. Those who deserve my thanks know who they are. More than anyone or anything, I'd like to thank God for making all this possible. I'm not religious in the traditional sense, but I do believe in miracles and a higher power, and without that power, I would not be here today.

Last but not least, thank *you*, reader, for your time and your companionship during this read. I wish you the best.

To conclude this note, I'd like to clear up some potential confusion for acquaintances who were visitors of my old website and recognize some of the poems from there. The following poems appeared on that website prior to the publication of this book. Some have been revised for this work. To view the original artwork and read these poems' earlier forms, please visit *https://www.kaylacookauthor.com/p/archives.html.*

"Dusk" (2021)
"One-Sided" (2021)
"The Night Queen" (2020)
"The Dark Forest" (2020)
"Will You Be There?" (2020)
"Reaching Out" (2021)

"Dirge of the Found" (This began as a school project many years ago. Essentially, I had to create original lyrics to accompany an existing tune. I've made many modifications since to help it stand alone. It was published on my website in 2020.)

"The World Weeps with Me" (2020)

"Ascension" (2021)

"Ocean Song" (2021)

"Dawn: A New Door Opens" (The original name of this poem was "A New Door Opens," and a variation was originally published under my alias "Allerion" on Writing.com in December of 2018. It was then republished on my website in 2020.)

ABOUT THE AUTHOR

Kayla S. Cook is a writer, a visual artist, and a book hoarder with a dark sense of humor and a deep love of nature, oversized sweaters, and symbology. Books and other art forms have long been her sanctuary. It is her dream to provide for others the solace, understanding, and inspiration that so many creators have provided for her.

www.ingramcontent.com/pod-product-compliance
Lightning Source LLC
LaVergne TN
LVHW050923210926
848482LV00012B/520
9798995031208